Starting School

Fiona Pragoff
Story by Peter Heaslip

METHUEN CHILDREN'S BOOKS

Lucy woke up early. Today was very
special – her first day at school. She
had been to nursery but would big
school be different? Would she like
it? Lucy wondered.

Her sister Jo was still asleep, so
Lucy tickled her and woke her up.

They both went
to the bathroom
and had a wash,
then Jo helped
Lucy to get
dressed.

Lucy was so excited she ate hardly any breakfast. Mum had made her a sandwich to eat at playtime. "You might feel hungry then," she told Lucy as she did her hair.

When it was time to go, Dad saw them all off. "I'll pick you up in the car after school," he said as he kissed Lucy goodbye.

Lucy, Jo, Mum and the dog set off for Lucy's first day at school.

When they got there Lucy's friend Ben and his mum were waiting for them.

The teacher remembered her and smiled. "You came to visit us and played in the home corner, didn't you?" she said.

While Ben and Lucy's mothers gave the teacher the dinner money Ben showed Lucy where her name was on the register.

"Take Lucy and tell her where to hang her coat," the teacher said to Ben.

"Here's your peg," he said, "next to mine."

Ben showed Lucy the girls' toilets. "But don't go in *there*," he said, "that's the boys'."

Lucy's mum stayed at school for a while and helped some children with their painting.

Lucy was busy playing with the
other children and she didn't mind
at all when her mum went home.

Then Lucy looked around the room for something else to do. She built a tower with Ben and his friends. It was so tall that it came crashing down with a terrible noise!

Playing with the little bricks was much quieter and it was fun too, especially with a new friend.

At playtime
Lucy put on her
coat and went
outside to eat
her snack.

She found Ben and they sat on the
bench together.

When all the children came inside, Lucy played with the sand for a while.

It was just like nursery but there were too many children there, so she found a quiet place and sat down and did some lotto on her own.

The teacher called Lucy to play with the musical instruments. They all made a lovely noise. It was great fun!

Everyone had to get changed for PE.
Lucy was glad that she could
undress herself.

PE was great, but climbing on the
frames and jumping off was best of
all.

After they had changed back into their clothes it was time to wash their hands for dinner.

Lucy was a bit worried about school dinner in the big hall, but as it was her first day, her teacher sat beside her. She helped Lucy cut up her meat.

Lucy chose her pudding by herself. Her teacher chose the same pudding, and they both had lots of custard.

After lunch
was over,
Lucy and her
new friends
went outside
to play.

It had been so noisy outside that
Lucy enjoyed sitting quietly with
the children while the teacher read
them all a story.

When it was finished Lucy wanted to talk with the teacher, but she was busy with the older children so Lucy chose a book of her own to look at.

Lucy and a new friend sat down together to look at the book.

Lucy hadn't done painting yet so she went to the paint table and started a picture. Her teacher came and wrote her name on it. "I can write my own name," Lucy told her.

"Do you think we can write a story about your first day at school then? Come on let's try," her teacher said. She wrote the words first, and Lucy copied them.

There were lots of other things to do, but it was nearly time to go home. Already the other children had started packing up and tidying away all the things.

Jo had come to collect her. "Hurry up, Dad's waiting outside," she said.

Lucy couldn't wait to tell him what
she had done at school.

Dad was waiting for them outside
the gate. Lucy showed him her
painting and the book she was
taking home.

At home Lucy talked non-stop about school. She was still talking

about school when she and Jo
had a bath that night.

In bed while she was having a story she suddenly remembered, "I wrote a story at school today, but I forgot to bring it home."

"Never mind," said Mum, "you can remember it tomorrow and then we'll put it up on your bedroom wall."